An Undercurrent of Jitters

An Undercurrent of Jitters

CAROL LEVIN

MoonPath Press

Poetry
ISBN 978-1-936657-38-4

Cover photo: Carol Levin

Author photo: Dale M. Peterson & Theresa Elliott

Design: Tonya Namura using
Bellota (display) and Minion Pro (text)

MoonPath Press is dedicated to publishing the finest poets
of the U.S. Pacific Northwest.

MoonPath Press
PO Box 445
Tillamook, OR 97141

MoonPathPress@gmail.com

http://MoonPathPress.com

To Geo Levin.

*Since our wedding day we have been
learning and teaching marriage and love
to each other, expanding our lives,
confronting ways to muddle through
some craggy cliffs
to discover we are more
incandescent together
than ever we could have imagined.*

Acknowledgments

My sincere thanks to the publications in which these poems first appeared, sometimes in a slightly different version.

Confident Music Would Fly Us to Paradise: "So Very Married" and "The Reason We Keep Secrets"

Gloria Mundi Press: "Think Blue Pools and White Lilacs"

Just Bite Me (anthology of Humor, from Poet Works Press): "A Guest Will Arrive at Midnight"

The Literary Nest: "Swallowed My Regrets" and "Mail-Ordered"

OVS Magazine: "The Reason We Keep Secrets"

The Poetry Box: Love Poems Anthology: "Surfing Like a Carpet Tack Under the Influence of a Magnet"

Red Rooms and Others: "The Most Important Thing to Save When the House is Burning Down"

I am indebted to the friends and strangers who generously offered stories that inspired many of these poems.

Thank you Lori A. May for a close reading and perceptive feedback on the manuscript.

And many thanks to Vicki Ford, Janet Sekijima, Ruth Brinton, Francine Walls, and Katie Tynan for brilliance, advice, along with good natured discussions about all aspects of poetry.

Then my heart is filled with gratitude to MoonPath Press, to Lana Hechtman Ayers, and book designer, Tonya Namura for providing a home for this collection with the *super-moon-path-light* that illuminates it.

Table of Contents

Author Introduction

I was catapulted into this "project" before I knew it was going to be a project when I wrote a poem in response to James Galvin's "On the Sadness of Wedding Dresses." As I read his poem I realized I didn't know what my mother wore at her wedding or when the wedding was, or where, or who was there.

Then I couldn't stop thinking about it and began asking people if they knew how their parents met (deciding to give a space that could be less intrusive than asking them about their own meetings and marriages). Stories came pouring in.

Once each story began, the storyteller and the listeners were changed, along with the atmosphere in the room, providing me with prompts for poems celebrating the fact that each of us has a story relating to the subject of marriage or weddings, or the lack of them: our own, our parents, friends, and relatives.

This led me to research facets of marriage within: laws, history, culture, rules, religion, commerce, gender, expectations, outcomes, and personal *dramas*.

An Undercurrent of Jitters

Section One

I cannot fix on the hour, or the spot, or the look, or the words, which laid the foundation. It is too long ago. I was in the middle before I knew that I had begun.

—Jane Austen, *Pride and Prejudice*

Swallowed My Regrets

Ladylike in the mores of 1955
If you committed sexual intercourse
You were sentenced to marriage

A Commoner (Once Upon a Time)

Of course it wasn't
London's golden royal
marriage carriage but it was big,

old. Broken heater spewed
agitation uniting an angry
sun radiating heat from
asphalt all the way to Las Vegas

from Los Angeles—
a Saturday morning July 2nd
our eyes peeled to elude
flashing blue and red sirens of law,
erroneously assuming the Mann Act
meant any male conveying underage
females over state lines.
But I was about to be a bride.

Of course there were
no ladies-in waiting
waiting in the hour's long
line for a license
that holiday weekend,
no makeup, just
melted lipstick, a skirt
rushed over blue-flowered
summer shorts,
then the dash to the line
at the Justice of the Peace.

"Marryin' Sam Mendosa"
and his two sweating secretaries.
What, no Cardinal, no Bishop
witnessing I do's?

Of course no princess' tiara
over that crumpled blouse, no
royal prince with epaulets,
no giving

away father, no dowry or balcony
kiss, no air
conditioning or traditional
wedding-night romance,
no nuptial longevity after this scorched
once-upon-a-time
our offspring never know.

Was There a Veil in the Void That Came Before Me?

On the Sadness of Wedding Dresses
—poem by James Galvin

Until this moment
Until I began
to read . . . *On the Sadness* . . .
As Galvin asks: *"Where*
    is your mother's
    wedding dress,
    What closet?
    Where is your grandmother's
    wedding dress?
    What, gone?
    Eventually they all disappear . . .
I never ever
wondered, strange
to say, what
Mother and soon
gone Father
wore, or where,
who was there,
or even when
they married.
How could I
have forfeited
a chance
to ask?

My about-to-be
mother met my
about-to-be
father at her Aunt
Fannie's estate.

An unfamiliar bed
of roses for the odd
couple, a party
maybe catered.
Mother smiles
from my
photo, clicked
on my day,
my groom.
James Galvin:
     you say, *A few*
     lucky wedding
     dresses get worn
     by daughters—just
     once more,
     then back to the closet.
Fumbling buttons
I promise
family research,
get naked,
chilled, then tug
a plebeian
cotton elevated
to an activity
never fashioned for,
over my head, smooth
out bulges. Freed
from expectations
it's not sad.
It's white.

My Skin Wants to Be Rescued

    from a ruched bodice in stretch charmeuse,
freed to swirl in cold air, wants
    out of an organza tiered ruffled skirt
to feed on sunlight after
    a lace-up-front silk shantung
taffeta, with sleeves.
    My skin wants to burst
from a sweet-heart neckline. My
    smothered epidermis wants to abscond
from black satin, slip out of the empire
    waist sash, fly
from a silhouette of button-up-the-back,
    above a sweeping ivory train. Hot, my skin
with its dermis subcutaneous, drapey
    in front under flowing
chiffon in back—seethes. My skin,
    as seasoned as a fine stringed rosewood
finger-board, craves fondling. Stripped
    of its crinkles, black skin raffia
and caucasian seashell, skin seeks
    to shed the satin face
organza mimicking sky and clouds in oceans
    of champagne ripples tinged blush-pink
teased with naked silk florets. Skin
    to pet, touch, rub, taste. Skin
sweating under fern-green tulle flowers
    with asymmetrically graduated pleats,
swirling, swelling. Finally, out of a chic, cerulean
    liquid lamé, my skin's suddenly
unveiled from a gown of silver Spanish moss.
    The skin dilates between

the membranous branches of my legs, its vows
    exaggerate smoothness
under the damp summit
    of the groom, groomed bare.

Oh Romance

They met: in the supermarket cereal aisle
talking Cheerios. He realized he'd known her in grade
school playing tetherball and remembered she'd beat him.

And, They met: convulsed in pain in a Texas
military hospital on Christmas eve when the whole staff
was off merrymaking and as the duty nurse, she phoned
for the physicians who were still sober, read them the riot
act to get back and in emergency surgery he died and was
resuscitated, recovered after four months on her ward,
then he shipped out. Years passed, he served his tour. One
day she looked

up, he was standing there, for her, not what she expected
their daughter says. The daughter says her mother saved
his life that Christmas. And, They met: at their
wedding. Not an Indian classic three-day style wedding,
and not a "love match" but she and her bridesmaid's hands
were embroidered with intricate henna designs and she
wore red but not a sari, and he did not enter on a white
horse but her family told her they'd picked him to keep
traditions of ancestors together, told her not to expect too
much. Her grandsons roll their eyes, retelling the story.

And, They met: his son says how his father always
swore his mother "was the most beautiful girl in their
town and he wasn't going to marry anyone else!"

And, They met: on her summer break. She wrote
me from a village on the Adriatic, grumbling about how
her family made it clear he wasn't of their rank so he and

she, after dark, snuck away and swam almost a mile,
every night, to a small island and made love all summer.
They couldn't speak a word of each other's language.
The next summer she left her students, crossed oceans
back to that old family home with its dirt streets and the
gossiping, and married him. From the street below their
window I could hear her, on my visit years later, a village
woman's chirpy voice filled my ears with the foreign
sounds of Serbo-Croatian as though she'd never in her
life grown up as a California girl.

Then, We met: blind date. Before the door opened
and we landed our first look at each other both wondered
would this evening be like so many when we'd wished
we'd stayed home with a book.

Into the Rain

His dog started it. I reached to pat her
in the garden by Telegraph Hill's tower.
I missed my canines that summer,
he mentioned his wife
and how she died.

Walking together talking
of mates, mine home in Seattle
and his. I thought of my friend

even more states away, her widowhood,
the quality of kindness each
possessed and how in the world
to introduce San Francisco to Salt Lake City.

The only way it could have been arranged
was by the heavens, the light after death glow,
although, they are convinced
I was the mastermind.
He worried about rain. Year after year
declined invitations for a Seattle visit. Finally
his business compelled him here.

Of course only those heavens could have occasioned
the coincidence of her arrival that exact date.
Innocently each house guest hauled
suitcases to upstairs rooms
before the common quality of their eyes
met across the sweep of our dining room table.
That moment I remember, it was raining.

Convergence, Cake Candles, and
Talk About Time

Do you know how your mother and father met? No, silence, no.
Softly he speaks. We hear he was born to sharecroppers,
as a young child pricked

by cotton cones, the economy and subjugation. He holds sway
    and we relish envisioning his childhood under
wings of grandparents, guesstimating how, at fifteen,
    he felt when his voice was changing.

We are dazzled by the acclaim of his university days, his
    passions and capacities. We celebrate his birthday
of birthdays at his table tonight laid with a feast
    meatier than all the storylines of our lives.

He doesn't know how his father and mother met, he doesn't
    know the date they married. He slips us a secret
learned late about their marriage and we have
    been gifted a bond linking our lives, laughing
at versions of our exes,

of our tender spouses, of our weddings, and celebrations
    celebrating ourselves.
I said, "You've had such an interesting life"
    and in sequined sounds
he says, "Everyone has." Before we knew it we were
    revealing more—

in limbo like stilt walkers or giving into the hole of
    sadness climbing out with a layer
of thick skin never expressed before, seeing ourselves
    new in the flickering
of each other's eyes just before lit candles of time are blown
    away.

World-War-Two Armed Forces
Loved USO Dances

These boys are shuffled like bingo balls,
    based at a small Texas town.
A church recreation room, crammed with a confetti
    of strangers, air an undercurrent of jitters,
soap, sweat, starched new
    warrior uniforms fated for combat.
One of a swaggering group eyeing young
    female's fresh faces mentally prunes
off blooms one by one

    leading to one
whose heart under her ironed ruffles
    pounds at a touch of his hand
toward the dance floor then adrenaline
    surges when feet
find a one-two-three-four *"I'll Be Seeing*
    You . . .-two-three-four
You'll Never Know Just
    How Much I . .one and two-three-four.
Heated handfuls of hope
    elude the USO rule:

daredevil, he whispers close to her ear,
    "Will you see me again tomorrow?"
Without a smile she eyes him, a long look,
    "Get rid of that bush above your lip."

&, he did. Next day, she did,
    & hung on a long time across the world's
bloodshed counting one, two, three, four,
    gold stars of grief in windows down her street.

Holding him tight, she triumphed one and a two
    always the sassy dancer
with a flutter of red confetti
    throughout their years, zigging
        & zagging as bygone events do

   one
     step
       at a time

Change Comes Piecemeal

. . .married women lack independent souls
—Tennessee legislature, 1849

His wife was his,
an existence apart
her property was his,
his property was his,
his salary his business,
his, his will, inheritance,
his appetite for sex

and his wife, all his.
His *misses*, addressed
only by his name
first and last, his, but
to name his offspring

his name—
there: she
was valuable, if
she bore him
a boy.

Mail-Ordered

Thanks to the internet, men can see potential brides
online right now
        —HRF.org

—I can only stare as she says—

paid he wants
I fly we marry
falls for my photo

—I feel it in my eye
as tangled as knotted tinsel
in a visualized future,

mash my lips to calculate
a bride price.
I swallow watching

frothy clouds embraced
in sky—I fly
longing to interpret as she
above a whisper says,

no, no,
no afraid,
he wants, we marry

—my
heart thumps—

as wind rises
landing
she moves

delivered.

Rooms Concealed Doesn't Mean They Don't Exist

And there, at Topkapi Palace in Istanbul
    we weren't allowed
to tour the Ottoman sultans' wives' harem
where concubines were confined where
brides resided along with slaves
as well as everyone's family.

    We walked without a sign
of wives, display after display room to room
examining all sizes and shapes of gems embedded
in daggers, swords, and incised silver armor.

    Epoch-making men lived here,
men with wives, concubines, and slaves.

The main wives, those taken
into marriage to consolidate personal
and dynastic alliances
    were *free women*. Rare exceptions.

The sultan's mother
    ruled.
All knew well, love
was not a reason to marry.

Wiping Apocalypse Off On Your Elbow

Did you think marriage
was *The* wedding
a domestic prize
a future to obtain

did you think
it was pets with pie

that it was a career
acquiring a helpmate

that it would rewrite the void
geographic and factual
between mars and moon
the same as the distance
between your father
and your mother

did you think

between pie, ironing, and toilet
scrubs you'd unwind with books
could stay-at-home
boning up
on a career
bedding out domestic
plants'
frilly petals

you thought

there was no other course
of course

you thought this
is how we live

Without Consent

The silence lay leaden on the plates
in-between moments of conversation
camouflaging distaste for the groom,
for the new nuptials, for vows
covertly clinched, hours ago divulged as fact.

Not Uncle Syd, not Aunt June
not Evelyn and not Nana
and especially not Father
and more especially not
Mother and her husband Harry
who in a twist of fate happened

to be traveling through.
Not one of them lauding, but,
doing their best pantomiming
glass-lifting to newly-weds.

Family laps with paltry napkins
politely sitting, strung along
the curved off-yellow naugahyde
booth at the *Rib Pit*, Denver, Colorado's
exuberantly celebrated barbecue.

Grandma's Antediluvian Cut

Not the moment for anything negative.
I've never been a diamond person
so when he speaks I nod and envision

his little pebble of a single solitaire
as a wedding ring. Not a time
to be negative I remember, so

filled with butterflies but silent
I surreptitiously groan for
a wide band, silver, trimmed in gold

around inscribed serene initials.
After dessert I sit reflecting on today's
completely unexpected

turn-of-my-life event
as he mumbles back in his bedroom.
I wait concocting a response that appears

agreeable but decisive whenever
the gem makes its debut. Out comes
an old sock. Out of the sock tumbles,

like a ballroom's mirrored
disco-ball light, strobing
into an ocean of wild stars,

wind, and waterfalls' laughing
from fifty-eight hand cut facets:
our future,

a skyrocket at its apex
encircled in an antique filigree setting.
The first time I ever

comprehend the meaning,
takes your breath away.

Easy Do-It-Yourself Nup

Don't wait
        until you are ready
        to walk an aisle—
        additional clauses,
        estate issues,
        support,
        signing guides,
before lights bumble

scatter love
        in different languages,
        full name of future
        wife full name of future
        husband (comes first)
        a plan to preserve
        trust,
family ties, and inheritance—

who will be entitled
        shared debts
        nibbling softly an ear lobe
        procrastinating,
        assessed, in the event
        of a separation,
        lists before
        you blurt out elaborate
        pleas & appraised property
sized up ahead—

pre-nup backs up bifurcation
        to send plums of silvery
        moons reeling rubbing
        limbs inconspicuously

under the table, get
on with it while
memorizing
in a fueled heartbeat
the time his lips
first set fire to yours,

just smile,
        listing shared
        property next to—
You Paid How Much!!!!

facing financial agreements
        of dubious events,
        bell weather
        of wellbeing,
        while tears
        fill his eyes and
        she's deeply touched
        by monetary and emotional
        security in the nuptials
pre-nup

everything turns out alright.
(shocked and shy)
        Nup it like a bud
        blossoms before
        bride is bound
and groom grounded

My First Bridegroom Taught Me to
Iron His White Dress Shirts

Anticipate the paradisal smell the moment you wiggle
                                        its nose
straight-shot into a sleeve pleat. Unpucker, then swerve
                                        and curve folds
slipping into satisfaction. Instant gratification is the
                                        gratification

of steam, pressure, and finger's tactile fulfillment. Benefit
                                        of the set-up
flattening along the board's pointed end, spread open laid
                                        bare expecting
the hot fluster of steam from holes in the iron's flat side.
                                        Articulating,

the prima donna glide of wrist orchestrates a whisper of
                                        fabric transforming,
as though, next, rumpled crows feet and laugh lines are
                                        within
the imperium of your irrefutable authority hot against
                                        wrinkles.

The Reason We Keep Secrets

The ambrosia beetle makes holes,
chews trees silently. The pinholes

suck in rainwater to configure
layers so no two maples

are alike when sliced a thirtieth
of an inch thick for veneer.

Figured-ash veneer looks like eyes,
measled-walnut, like lips.

Satinwood is smooth like a good talker
inviting fingertip caresses.

Pearwood and wenge are mysterious.
A facade of veneer hides substrate,

top layer of intricate inlay obscures paradox.
No two husbands are alike.

The children ask about their father,
the husband who came before the present

husband, the one whose death
left a coil of personas hidden

under flitches of falsehoods. Layers
deeper than the silence of insomnia nights

below the story never learned.
What can I say? I worry,

chewing over Voltaire's adage,
"The secret of being boring is to tell everything."

Today's husband works wood, veneers his layers
delicately polishing with his hands all he touches.

He sorts and counts to join grains
verbose as fretwork.

While Watching One Half of the Show on the Anthropology Channel

I've caught it in the middle.
Subtitles explain—Some
tribe some country unfamiliar.

His two wives rip hair & pummel
each other. It says he says, "It would
exacerbate their angst if he intervened."

So a neutral interrupter disentangles
& none of them are wearing more
than a diaper type garment—

Starting with not enough
information is like sitting
on one end of an empty teeter-totter.

It says he says, "Now that they've been
calmed, he privately meets with each
wife." Asks, "What's the story here?"

That prods my own memory—
when I, Employee Grievance
Mediator, asked quarreling staffers questions.

At the point I laid bare
their problems & saw through their eyes
I understood each side of each outrage.

Our family of workers
sought resolution & calm,
if not attained: over crisp nurses

whites, sterile scrubs, or business suits
they slipped into their coats & quit.
Always, something left unsaid.

Then my employer had a problem
at what was dubbed a *family enterprise*
caring for those who are ill.

Later the three come
together as the husband tells it,
he & his wives talk as candidly

as cool liquid flows
down a mountain.
It says he says, "Each agrees

which wife is the incendiary wife,"
it says he says, "As husband,
it is his job

to set the amount she must
pay up as her fine."
Which part of his story

is naked truth? What I see
through his eyes is in translation. It's
understandable only half of the half, is my half.

Research "Wading Through a
Perfect Flood of Tears"

*Sisters, do you wish to make yourselves happy? Then
what is your duty? It is for you to bear children...
are you tormenting yourselves by thinking that your
husbands do not love you? I would not care whether
they loved a particle or not ...*
—Prophet Brigham Young

To take on various states of matrimony
I verb and I noun
transcend stamina and endurance
untighten fists of imagination—
this one's not easy
for me—to inhabit
an imagined role
within polygamy.
Husbands, I read, are asked
by "virgins" to be added
as brides to their
burgeoning families.

> *if any man espouse a virgin, and desire to espouse
> another, and the first give her consent, and if he
> espouses the second, and they are virgins, and have
> vowed to no other man, then he is justified."*
> *Doctrine and Covenants,*
> Section 132, verse 61

Husbands "it's said"
are "required"
to acquire permission

of the current wives before
they add one more.

    But the first wife will say, 'It is hard for I have lived
    with my husband twenty years, or thirty, and have
    raised a family of children for him, and it is a great
    trial to me for him to have more women.'

In my scene I rehearse:
braiding my hair and braiding
my child's as well. Pantomime
a day full of pronouns in states
of domesticity all, *her, they, we,*
she, in the ill appointed "family"
where much is to be done, hour
after hour and occupies
unsubstantiated guesses.
Until I get to the question every
one wonders about. Turns for a jab to procreate?

    Joseph Smith was married to at least 12 women prior
    to July 12, 1843

I have worked to place
myself in this place by
imagination
only. Makes me sneak
away holding my
clothes wound in a small
bundle.
What would the taste
in my mouth
taste like? To speak
my verbs meeting

nouns are not dutiful. I've
no *sense memory* for a scenario
enough to place me in that place.

> *A few years ago one of my wives, when talking about*
> *wives leaving their husbands said, 'I wish my*
> *husband's wives would leave him, every soul of them*
> *except myself.' That is the way they all feel, more or*
> *less, at times, both old and young.*
> —Prophet Brigham Young,
> *Journal of Discourses*, v. 9, p. 195

Rules

(1)
Weddings go unmentioned in the bible.
The daughter's father says that's that.
And "that" means a link to sow
economically, socially, tribal seeds
from the fruit of wily matched loins.

(2)
Dangling before us the familiar uncomfortable silence:
If anyone can show just cause why this couple cannot
lawfully be joined . . .
    Did you hear?
A shout from the back wall: *Bigamist?*
A cry from the balcony: *under age?*
Grandma wails: *He's her uncle!*

(3)
Do you take this person . . . the only compulsory question.
Do you take this person for: Wife/Wife, Husband/Husband,
Wife/Husband, Husband/Wife, Woman/Husband,
Man/Wife? Yes, before lips plug-in an airtight kiss.
Salud, Skål, L'Chayyim and Cheers clinking
to life, to health, to joy, and high fives round.

(4)
(A few states require consummation of the marriage
through sexual relations to make it official.)

(5)
Witness: you sign the certificate, swear you watched
with your own eyes—All contracts require an onlooker's
autograph. No one can pretend then the marriage didn't
happen—Some places, when you swear, it means you know
one or both are virgins, or in the case of a remarriage,
you affirm they have not slept together or with anyone
since the loss of their previous spouse.
Quakers ask all present at a wedding to sign as witnesses.

(6)
A *Witness* and an *Officiate* are another absolute rule.
The rest of the occasion of your wedding is yours
to choose—sing songs, say poems sanctified or silly,
pray, blow bubbles, on a cliff, a cathedral, a pagoda,
a park, a parlor, a full on
adrenaline rush, a thriller. Of course a thriller!
I might as well say it after the: *show just cause*
why . . . the suspended silence
then takes a breath, and rings manifest
as nectar for the love birds. A link
to a biblical *fruit of their loins.*
"Speak now or forever hold your *peach*." And that's that.

Flash Back

After Benji, that stifling summer
day chuckled to his friend
man to man (my man)
both eyeing me
said "oh yeah get em young
keep em barefoot and pregnant"
I was expected, and did,
laugh,
so young that day I thought
he was joking.
I remember it was summer,
hot,
I was barefoot. Feet bare.
Who would ask
if they were burning?

Papa Forbade College for the Girls
So They Would Be Good Wives

she said,
starting the story backwards,
before I gasped
after she emphasized she was seventh,
her eyes meeting mine, saying
there were eleven
eleven children, all together,
and then she told me, while
I stood agape my own body
slumping in trembling exhaustion
taken-up remembering joie de vivre,
then the ravages after childbirth
and child rearing, as I surmise pandemonium
of boys, girls, teens, toddlers, sucking
infants, skinned knees, dirty diapers, daily
meals, and pregnant too?
She twinkled then flashed a cunning
smile and talked about
the business her mother
also ran.
By then I was breathing hard
it was all too hard for me
but she, knowing, it would
be a great ending finished
me off by saying
when her mother was still a maiden
two brothers courted her,
she dearly loved the younger
but calmly married
the elder,
the heir, who would inherit
their famous father's bulging
bags of money and everything else.

Late Late Late On Tuesday

Nine month baby bulge
wheeling hairpin curves
mountain cabin to town
to the appointment
to marry at 11.
In the rush you remember you forgot
a ring
snap up
a slender
silver band
that needs sizing
holding the almost
two-year olds hand
as time bolts
you beg the sphinx-
like jeweler
"h u r r y."
His black eyes
narrow
eyeing the runny
nose of the
little boy
the volume
of the unborn
baby
the shifting
from foot
to foot
bridegroom
the already
ticked-by time
and casually

he says
to you
*lady what's
your hurry?*

Import Shop, Victoria, Vancouver Island

He'd stopped by the shop before. She was a tourist
    attracted by exotica.

His first words amid wildly patterned colors, dyed,
    woven, embroidered

were a question: *are you Jewish, your feet have Semitic
    curves?*

She appraised undomesticated dark eyes, black beard,
mis-matched jodhpurs and cape

her first words also question: *are you an artist?*

Spring thaw scattered wild flowers, the fancy answer was
    she moved to Canada

to the art of a soft-spoken man, with big trees and
    exquisite hands,

she dreamt water-wheels, ferris wheels, effervescent
    dense green seedlings,

before she conceived of the mystery of kissing under
    spangled sky bustling with busy

guardian angels sewing lace in the air, emptying sacks,
    unlocking latches.

Her New York mother and grandmother applauded her
    an ovation

as a delicate life force waited in the lobby-of-the-universe

to take hold by virtue of the unsuspecting pre-purposed
    pair:

artist man, fleet footed woman, the effort necessary

not more, never married, just distant friends fulfilling the
    set-up

so the daughter could slip into her conduit

"and come through."

Oh So Many Views, Attitudes, Opinions, Beliefs

Orthodox Jewish tradition encourages modesty,
beauty is a divine gift according to Jewish scholars
and when a woman marries that beauty is private,
kept private by covering her hair with a wig.

A point of view by some scholars
    is that wedded women's hair covering
is not an obligation of biblical origin.
    A different mixed bag of scholars and dedicated
rabbis are ready to portion out punishment

for gazing at women. This is a mandate according
    to the bible, or a decree according
to the rabbi:
    "From your marriage day conceal your hair or risk
terrible disease, give up your hair for God." Some say
    it is determined in the Talmud.

The Talmud, or the bible, or the rabbi threaten women
    not covering elbows, collarbones and knees, they
argue over how much skin can be exposed. At the
wedding
    Hasidic brides' faces are blotted out by opaque cloth.
Wedding guests see only the dress.

The rabbi, the Talmud, the bible execrate behaviors
    that are grounds for divorce such as appearing
in public with loose hair. When you're a wife it's a must
    to shroud every stray strand. This authority says this,
that group says that, another decides hair covering is

determined by the community. One says rabbis define
    hair as sexually erotic and prohibit men from praying
in sight of a woman's hair. Have you heard some say
    a man's not allowed to hear

a woman sing, and not allowed in a confined area
    where women are present outside of close family?
But what about elevators? Some say ok for
    30 seconds, others say never, elevators can
get stuck. So after

marriage only the husband may see his wife's hair
however
    Hasidic brides shave their head, well some do, or
many
        others used to

although some husbands and wives take over their own
lives
    and make their own rules and walk together, sing
        together,
ride up and down floor after floor and, divinely happy,
    pray together.

Fancy-Dressed As a Faux Grownup

Always fancied a pianist had perfect teeth
and writers, bright white margins,
conjured astrophysicists with brain-waves
of teased out patterns of planets. High school
good-girl, my world, fastidiously folded.
He was *goodbye* Henry. I was seventeen.

Musicians have cubism in sound so that
dancers' hands take on the color,
explore elliptic edges of distance.
Today picturing my pale, frail adolescence
luck has curly hair the same way
I laugh all over myself confessing

my finger fluttered a baby diamond.
Memory's forgotten the moment
like in the movies, Henry B. said *marry me.*
I know my color, *-virginal-happy-ever-after*
sighed. Engaged. A sanctuary.

First fox trot, prom night Darrin D.
cut in, took me in his arms, planets
burst into flame, shattering white edges
of the music, sound of drum's percussion
explosive enough to curl hair lead me to fling
the little ring like a rainbow in a gale.

Section Two

Love is a new relative to the long history of marriage.

—Anon.

Pop the Question Poppycock

Is considering marriage
    so slight a thought
        you *pop* the question?
            (Sounds) so unconsidered

surprising as a salted
    corn kernel burst into bloom,
        popped into a mouth,

someone hoping yeses
        in colors of *pop* art,
            popped it on one knee,
                popped will you marry
me, just *popped* out
and *popped* the bubble—
        Popped it in an e-mail,
            popped it in a song, on
                an airplane banner
                    or in a bouquet of white
                        bearded iris,

popped it on the beach,
    popped it on the bed
        even though pooped
            it *popped*, what do you hear?
                Pop pop pop silly eh?

Soda-pop suggests not quite *popping* it
    the fathers, our pops *pop*—when Dads wed,
        bulging eyes often described as popping
            and baseball bats hit a short high fly,
                popsicle, then Pop Goes the Weasel—
                the old country dance.

Pop-the-question is always
only one question
(in case you were asking).

The End of a Four-Year Engagement

Edgy as a runner at the mark early
on Jan 2nd to sign-up
for Seattle city park's summer
wedding dates. Landed the park
twelve blocks from the house you say,
but "forgot to tell the Groom."

Pored over weather reports
for past Junes, agonized
over unreliable
previous forecasts then rented
bumbershoots from "Bella Umbrella"
solving a rain anxiety no one
had control of and under the actual
wedding day's

strobing sun each guest puffed-up,
in folding chairs on the burning brown lawn,
umbrellas, inflating a myriad of colors saving
the spectators from heat stroke.

A movie mad bride inspired by a procession
in *The Godfather*, you choreographed
a surprise parade envisioning *Fiddler On the Roof*.
"I'm not sure I understand
your vision" whispered the Groom.

After vows perked along, & at the curb
pedicabs arrived to ferry some guests, the entire
congregation rose in jubilant applause.
Flaunting parasols, one hundred people brimmed
the street to follow the Bride & Groom sashaying

downhill, neighbors cheering from windows & porches.
Violinists hidden all along the route, one by one
like *pied-pipers*, stepped in from behind bushes & fences

taking the lead, so as the procession proceeded the music
swelled. Celebrants suddenly realized the fiddling
musicians were talented children. An infectious joy
struck & stuck on 34th Avenue NorthWest
& to this day you struggle

to convince your spouse that you hear
bows singing their strings & the air filling
with magical melody every time you travel
the length of that park's capricious avenue.

Acting Like an Animal at the Wedding

But before giving your pet a starring role, think
about whether this will be an enjoyable experience
for him . . .Planning on dressing your pooch in a tux?
Make sure it fits properly.
—Essence Bridal Guide website

Tail's groomed—
the lead has strands
of gold
that keep slipping
but match
the rings
and complement
the family
style—

under the aisle
scents
of puppy treats
distract canine's
agonized ears

encourage
the processional—
Beethoven's
Ode to Joy

so to avoid
jolting
guests
with baying
traced to wolves'
warnings in the wild,

53

or a domesticated
dog's yowl
that trumpets

changing
circumstances—
or as wildlife
zoologists say, coyotes
celebrating
with maniacal laughter.

Spicy Frankincense, Myrrh and Riddles

"A weak man is a woman"
Old time aphorism, maybe
    still implied.
Can't say that
    about Solomon's
aggressive foreign
    relations.

I've heard
    King Solomon
had 700
    given to him
as international
    tokens
of friendship
    wives.

I've heard
    whispered
he kept 300
    concubines.
Then there's
    bible rumors of

gifts from
    the hairy footed Queen
of Sheba and
    about sexual
relations on her
    visit to
his court.
    Her spices,

she pronounced
    rolling syllables
on her
    tongue, were riddled
some gossips say, and exchanged
    for a son.
Still appreciated.

The Rescuers Said Most Glaciated Peaks Storm

Fist of her mate on its way
eyes like savage summer snow
a storm without a name
slowed down considerably
after thunder battered above an ear

like lightning lit over Karakoram Range
and finally degenerated outside the eye
at the height
of the ferocity—

Her skirt was bunched around her body
in the new morning
triumph of light
    snow ice and meltwater had roared down
    in avalanches
    on a woozy shrouded shoulder, as if
    Himalayan black gravel and mud sloughing
    in the armpit
    shaped crevasse,

    thrust her rocks
    to the surface   still proud
in abrogating high speed afternoon winds—
to become the center
of concentrated solitude.

The observer's intent on the shapes and ribs
of trouble in his mind
the objects of experience
and the present moment they can't
ever go back to. Then the next hard blow.

After Thanksgiving Friday

Feels like air has leaked slowly
from another bleak Friday day-after-turkey
day-off, as she and her also-single also
trying-to-animate-her life, friend, choose a local
supper club, and finger the white table cloth
and flattened linen napkins, swirling white wine
in champagne flutes: oh so sad they feel

so drained. A voice, an extreme Delaware un-
modulated accent out of nowhere asks her
for a dance, later he was out of town often, finally
he whispered breaking rules revealing his top
security CIA post swearing her to secrecy in his
extreme east coast pattern and pitch spreading
a tingle of drama she loved

and kept to herself except to tell her dear friend and their
other friend, all three agree, vow confidentiality.
The gals daily chatter in thrall of their pal wasn't
without suspicion as they sustained the secret but cast
about for more info, no internet then. Always his lavish gifts,
beyond her desk-job means, were lovely, she loved
them intoxicated by that cadence, inflection, the whispering
and the never knowing when he would return
from covert international assignments.

Secrets: an exciting edge to walk along. Then he was busted
his actual name the real one very ordinary
his real days all dull and commonplace his gaze cast aside
a whine in his voice he said his wife's name
and names of his babies, a year old baby boy

a two year old too and she felt her
breath and blood drain from her body.
He said, *wife*, as she noticed her own
heart spill out to the unknown stranger.

Departure

The bed's sweat wet sheets tangle my legs. I hug the quiet phone against my belly getting a grip on nausea. A neat row of big suitcases wait on the ugly turquoise rug. One for the happy boy, ten years old, one for the reluctant little girl, filled with dresses, summer, lightweights she hates. My suitcase crushes cool short skirts and a favorite red bikini, and his, his god dammed suitcase with its lid open, a groaning mouth, where piled slacks and t-shirts make me think of tongues, lying tongues shouldn't you say? We need to leave this room rolling the cases to a cab—rolling cases to security, rolling ourselves to the gate to enter the plane, all four all packed. Three a.m., three, he doesn't answer as I dial and mumble his name. Where is he, he took a woman home from my house at midnight after I told her he is not, notice I say not, it is an exclamation, not staying to marry her. He is packed, see that case, his underwear. She was hysterical. He took her home, said he'd be right back. We'd go hand in hand to the blue water bay, a black rock beach on a small island. We need to dress, need to leave soon I shout to the empty room. Where is he? I bought the plane, I bought the ship, I bought new shoes for the girl, the boy and for me. It cost a lot.

June Eighth Five Years After June Eighth
for Ruth

Five.
Red roses.
Fresh pressed
white linen.
White candles wick
white light. Two
chairs weighted.

Cool champagend
fingers love glistening glasses
toy with the chill.
Right arms, and eyes
raise, meet.

Best friends stood
bridesmaid and best man
before the fireplace.
Living room
walls candied with
Parker Paint pink.
Afternoon sun streamed
well wishes
and a minister
blessed.

Toast fifth anniversary
of arguments.
Concede alcohol hang-
overs the where-
were-you-last-
night's slugfests.
Sudden insight

when diamonds
swirl on her hand
as they lift their toast
to year five. Lift eyes

eye to eye to acknowledge
mismatched, a mistake.

Means to the End

In the witness box watching
the courtroom door admit a Mr. Mum tiptoeing
his way along the nearly deserted rows
of legal pews with a hammer in his hand,
I don't know who he is
in his black suit but I think
to myself: nail down another issue.
*****
Fall '77 we joined,
planted forests, children—
dug into text books, budded
and unfurled like ferns:
mist snuck between branches
of the days, years, widening
sighs into chasms and now
our roots detonate within this room.
*****
Lame-duck mother-in-law in Idaho swears.
Her hand raised
unseen, examined via speaker-phone.
Court-reporter taps to capture
the partisan voice cradling the son
and we rock remembering
the family you never get back.
Definition of dissolution:
everybody ends broke.
　　Oh boy you bet!
*****
I say, "I have measured the roundness of the earth by
　　unreimbursed expenses."
Personal property: this is stupid,
stop.

How did we get here you wouldn't . . . I didn't . . .
    This marriage.
I haven't asked enough.
*****
His beard looks like Mephistopheles. Pleading
to be an ex, sitting his turn,
boxed-in palm-up pledging
truth, then his lawyer's tactics ring
bells to push buttons:
average monthly income
after taxes, he intones,
bedrocks between seventeen-fifty below zero.
Landmark decisions never behave—
*****
During the drone of final
arguments an ant makes
his lazy way across a pew
aiming for the edge
no, now he turns
& goes the other way.

Indefinite Elastic Span: Interval, Duration, Hour, Minute, Second, Instant, Epoch

Measure and di-vide. Time
moves, but can't move slower
—can't move faster, time's toc and
tic is absolute. Our existence experiencing
time is proof of our unreliable sensory appreciation

reminding me how I confuse my zombies
with my vampires moving fast or moving slow, or,
how I watch a leprechaun shaped shadow flitting across
the rug and up the wall looking back motioning come,
    come—
    come on
    come-on catch up,
    as he benignly dissolves and
    I mark
    time
    waiting to be ok'd
by the judge in bitter weather, sitting tight

for the storm to release its sting after
ten uncountable years.   Time moves
apart, divorce ends that endless involvement.

    Snapping,
    I'm catching up. Wait!

Ex es

Theory reduction itself is divisible into three:
translation, derivation, and explanation.
—Alyssa Ney, *Reductionism*

How did this happen
bum
not
what
I
***
Three couples
soon
six x es
then six met

***

only
other xxx s
that's
reductive math
accumulating

Surfing Like a Carpet Tack Under the Influence of a Magnet

Gay dating sites, senior dating sites,
sites for widowed singles where
women can meet men,
Christian men and Christian women.
Jewish sites for divorced unmarrieds.
Sites for the affluent where they chat for hours
without paying sites. Then find dates
by intersecting zip codes, or matching professions
on gravitational attraction sites
emphasizing charisma, charm and eye-appeal.
Some fall in love on the site
where limber locals meet to dance. Lorna looked
at sites for Colombian techies and only found
Brazilian ladies and Costa Rican poets
for companionship. Some avoid sites fearing
flimflam, hoax and chicanery.

Arrange for gifts and flowers, ogle exotic
foreign beauties from hard to pronounce countries.
Browse Russians bearing vodka
with no accented language barriers.
Muscle-men's profiles work out on sites
with hard *six packs*.
One site is called *Luvfree*
with notes on how it works for *Beautiful People*
mixing their chemistry profile right in their laptops.
Lorna to her surprise
found love. Really. On
Amazon's *No-Name Wonders* site.

They are honeymooning
this morning and I'm left
with yesterday's cake,

sweet cake from the cake's top tier
under the allotropic tin site bride and groom

Wizardry of Pursuing Epiphany When Searching for a Mate

If you don't have two culinary disasters
     a week
you're not a creative cook. Archetype
of an unworthy fruitcake
     when writing
you read a lot
about reading.
No
     when reading
you read
a lot
about writing.
If you do not have two

literary catastrophes a week
     you are as bland
as a green winter grape,
probably
     for prowess

you need a stem load
of six or seven paramours, or
multiplying cycles
     of lovers
to refine like re-tuning pitches
of scales on the circle of fifths,
a Danny, a Henry, an Ed and a Ted,
years of wangling
a how, experiments terminating
     until overflowing
as though caught

within a chorus
of hundreds you
       lift off
into what we call
a fall
in love.

Planners Package Processional As
Slight of Hand

Full-service service or just a day of day-budgeted,
vendors, venues, mother-of-the-bride father-of-the-bride
groom-of the-bride mother-of-the-groom
father-of-the-groom bride-of-the-groom and what's
the difference, delegation of weight of details and savvy
planner's plans plans proceeding as planned contracts
contracted pre-wedding- wedding-wedding- post
wedding- plans all treated properly slowing or speeding
result of perfecting the package of expectations and
planning within financial residue, allocations, quotas
altogether fees forecast in statements, affordable after
rings are slipped after cake mowed down after flowers fly
after rice falls all recalled as a magic satire of planner's
aplomb run amok in colors of votives, wiggle room of
photographers, caterers, bartenders, and DJs, dozens of
job descriptions, myriads of tasks require voodoo, hairy
fairy dust, from church to church blessings of support offer
supernatural ability, finesse all day to day until basking in
the glow after the bill paid is preternatural, and Ms Planner
has a flop down feet up, amen, *it's a wrap.*

Something Gooey to Sweeten This World

lessons were fleeting stuck in the chinks of time between
    work

for a bride and groom astonished by their own emotion

on their way towards sleep, drifting on clouds lathered

in the largeness of their scale in dreams leading

them to the marshmallow yellow chicken farm

a new kind of holiday, a tendency toward giddy

as if they flew between the spires of the Taj

carbonated as colored crystals of glass in a kaleidoscope

On and On

When bubbles burst, new bubbles are born.
—Sinda N. Bhanoo, *New York Times*, June 15, 2010

This scientific report about bubbles insists
    it's the variable of the viscosity
that determines how long it takes before
    the globules rupture. As in, how thick
the matter is—like soapsuds from a dishpan
    of little breaths puffing or tension
across a bubble wand.

Until I read this report I thought the bubble's
    invisible last gasp was *it*. The report
argues otherwise. We erroneously see a bubble vanish.
    It rebirths itself in surface air trapped
in, what they call, *"reborn daughters."*
    A barely visible flock of pinhead
sized bubbles embroidered below: along the kitchen counter,
    living room rug, or tips of summer grass. We learn
to appreciate how matter
    is more tenacious than we assume. When

marriage ends with death the abandoned spouse
    "bursts by some instinct," cites another study,
"to carry-on." Impelled to feel how it felt when holding
    in his or her palm, the now departed one's daily
tools, stand, so to speak, in the lost loved ones shoes
    for a first time; scrubbing a kitchen, vacuuming,
or mowing the back yard's once foreign territory. For
    the first time crossing the identity barrier
to engender a hand to unscrew
    rigid jar lids, repair broken chairs and wax the car.

After the burst, energy bubbles-up buoyant
in the shape of a new future
    although it could be mistaken as perpetual silence
look again, embrace those little bubble babies reborn
    on old surfaces. It matters.

Anne Answers

Anne describes how her mother loved her husband
her entire lifetime. Six months after they wed, he died in
    the war.

Anne says not the husband who was her father, that came
later, after the new widow
went also to war, and grieved in uniform, saluting, to carry
on his steadfastness.

Anne says she poured over their letters when her mother
    passed,
the pre-war-love letters locked away during her mother's
    long life, cherished.

Anne tells us that from Normandy, long ago, she telephoned
    across the ocean
to her mother saying she was there,

stood on the beach, found his grave, her voice an
    intermediary
beaming over the waves to her mother. *Found him for you.*

Stealing My Grief

Possible her name was not Shelly. But true
she had Las Vegas long stripper legs. True
she was blond, tall as my father. Possible
she did not have a kidnapped little boy
in Mexico my Father footed the bill to find.
She spun spiderwebs of lies, he was
truly tangled in the silk
threads of her spell and the allure of her legs.

I was twenty-seven and knew nothing
of them until I truly needed his help
to bounce back
after my lover's lightning-out-of-the-blue
exit. Father sent a ticket to fly and spilled
the beans about Shelly, five years
my junior. Then *tied-the-knot.*
Shelly was my stepmother.

True, soon lies were laid bare, the marriage
annulled. My Father sent Shelly to me,
he said I could *help her,* then he died.

His crazed once-wife Shelly howled
water-works, as we flew to the Denver funeral.
I went all out to soothe her boo-hooing all day
all night and I think it was all a lie. By then
she had stolen my new beau
she had stolen my friend's diamond rings
she had stolen the rent I paid for her
and now, she was stripping me of that time
where loss spins no honest-to-goodness shape.

The Secular Jew Outsider Attends the Catholic Church

Nancy and I on the pew in the middle,
a mission to collect background
for our acting-class scene.
Whatever the priest said sprung
a tender nerve in Nan, turning
she said *gotta get out get out*
and we slid over laps
marched out the middle aisle, eyes turning
to glower at our impudent exit—

Nancy and I once more, on a punishing pew
where she aches today to turn
back time, resurrect Big Mountain, Montana,
flirting with her big man future
spouse, future father of her boys, future
meal maker, nurturer, coach, dog lover,
who despite not being wily at fiscal matters,
ever the passionate
supporter and adorer of all her
dreams and scenes except this

scene, a tolling bell nightmare
where Nancy and I sit pinned,
this time the priest by her side
on the front row pew
in a church she wants to escape.
Her man stowed within
the hard yellow-rose draped casket
slowly fetched up the center aisle.
Turning to me whispering
she says, *we were in the middle,*
we were planning more.

Hooked

It was a cosmic revelation the message that something has happened, his death maybe. Then, fully awake I remembered it was my dream. There had been death, and the death released me, freed from panic, from constant possibility of the house afire or police at the door. The primal instinct was to protect my boy and baby girl and it's not that he didn't care: he couldn't stop himself, exactly what I had felt sure I'd save him from, believing he would change for me, so sure I could delicately nurture and he'd heal when we wed. That was my dream, then. It took so long, and left little babies but finally we were freed. He was too. Everybody had done their best and it was impossible.

Crawling Through the Crannies of
My Brain Where They Say Everything's
Still Stowed

Ok let me ask you, what were you doing
in my dream? Never
can I remember you in a dream of mine not to mention
so flesh and blood absolutely alive. My gosh,
I can't even remember clearly what you looked like when
we were together. I haven't seen you in,
well, uncountable years. Did you choose now
because tomorrow is my,
and well
this is unbelievable too,
my forty-third wedding anniversary
and you and I had been divorced eons before
that sunny wedding day? And I remember
it has also been forty-three years
since the morning you died.
I didn't even comprehend this was a dream
while I was dreaming it,
and you, maybe,
were twisted by magnetic rays in the galaxy
at the moment in my dream I was celebrating
finding a perfect parking place and that never happens
while awake,
and the car fit snug against bull thistles and sweet peas and
stepping on the brake I heard chirping
locusts and crickets then I saw you. Jumped from the car
and called and called,
do you think I actually called your name out loud
in my sleep? You were wearing a summer weight tan suit
a bit wrinkled and I wasn't surprised
to be calling. Because I was dreaming

I didn't know I'd be rattled about it all day
today and
you didn't hear and
I called louder, faster,
but really, down deep,
I wasn't surprised
that you kept

walking
and never
looked back.

Day & Night

I talked to the Moon about tides.
　　　But Moon gave himself
all the best lines before
　　　I became enlightened,
before I found out
　　　it takes a team. Not exactly
cat-dog, cream-sugar,
　　　hand in glove.
It's Sun that amplifies half
　　　the ocean's inflations, forces
vigorous as the Radio City
　　　Rockettes kicking
on a regular schedule.
　　　Waves aren't airy nothings
rattling paradox,
　　　churning in the bay
sloshing up our bluff sighing
　　　years of stormy stories.
They spin themselves silly

to couple, moon and sun—
　　　a tightrope balance,
like a marriage
　　　on the gravitational field.
Very like marriage
　　　his lines—
and
　　　her lines—
when partners congruent in counterpoint
　　　generate forces
bringing to mind an undulating
　　　effervescence of articulation.

Notice of Death

He's not sick and he's not a writer
but my husband
is writing his own

obituary. Energy leaps him
every morning around
the lake exercising his old dogs.

Will he expose how crushed by grief
he is as one by one the dog family dies?
Will he treat you to his irresistible

laugh, confess he cracks-up
at my quips?
Will he accurately say

his heart is assaulted as I,
couldn't-care-less cavalier, kill
summer flies?

I'll bet he'll forget to reveal he helps
everyone at the speed of the sound
of "yes."

Impish raconteur, he'll recite the tale, one
of hundreds, how in a cloudburst he shoved
the butt of a St. Bernard up a sliding bank

to reunite her with her overwrought owner.
Surly he will say that the day he was born
he was born to own the sky,

addicted already to flight. And very likely
he'll not say he's not perfect.
Although I may be mistaken.

I want him to brag
from his grave
that he's a magician

who will live
on for ages in the art
he's created with wood.

He's not sick thinking over
how he will reflect
himself in the *Seattle Sunday Times*

to strangers scanning
the departed. Born:
day, year, place,

such and such
parents, graduated, worked,
traveled, belonged to,

sons, daughters, beloved . . .
no he won't say
the usual. Of course in the course

of reading obituaries
you discover only the good, die.

Keen to Do His Share of Marriage

Three dinners in succession, each serving six
brings food for thought.
Friday the therapist who's also a poet
and her periodontist
mate meet a counselor of

pregnant girls. They caress the host's
handmade woodwork then feed on breasts
of parmesan chicken as he mulls over
midnights scrubbing sticky piles of pans.

Saturday, a musician, a painter, a writer and a blower
of glass examine
raisins in curry on rice. Each
hash up family clashes, bestiality, first marriages.

Sunday, pot pie, two actors, an opera singer
and a diamond dealer delve politely
as possible the socially unacceptable
topic of religion. Quarreling, questioning
God's potency—one by one,
a menu of conclusions gyrate
apropos of this thing called *God*.
And why not—

The contrapuntal subject grumbles
past dessert's rum over ice cream.
Some offer that if there was
actually God God wouldn't be necessary.

Dinner plates ablutions drip and dishtowels dry
as he ponders and polishes each word, slips one by one
into his mouth to sample the fundamental essence of
    their taste.

A Guest Will Arrive at Midnight

He was plumping his pillow when she asked him to swap
the bulb blown out on the porch—
Said he: *tomorrow.* She: *A guest is arriving at midnight!*
Said he: *tomorrow!*
So she slid open the bulb bin to flush one out.
He, in one stride, one instant
was behind her glowering *OK I'll do it!* wrenching
the virgin bulb from her clasp, disagreeably
burrowing for another. She battered his back
shrilling—*you grabbed that from me!*
He grumbled, producing one lower in watts
she snatched it back—
Said she: *I'm doing this!* He stomped back to bed.
She fumed to the porch on the street, stool
in hand—remembered to switch the front door lock off,
stepped up in pajamas balancing her weight, fingertips
flying: she tilted her head
to look into the dark
unscrewing, scratching turn after turn—
extracted the orb, twittered it two times
like a baby rattling its toy,
stepped down, exchanged the old for new,
balancing again on the stool scratchily screwing
the new one in place she switched the blaze on:
returned stool, tossed burnt bulb out—glaring at him:
he back at her—
How they'll laugh at themselves later—counting
How many Levins
it takes to screw in a light.

Think Blue Pools and White Lilacs

A mangy pelt of grey incrementally closed-down the day
to kick up jaw-snapping whitecaps from the shoreline out
seven miles to the now obscured island. Whistles of wind
    oscillate
pitch and volume, circle and suck, push into the crannies
    of our cream
colored stucco which has withstood since the twenties,
    today
tested again. Tested like our marriage finally synthesized
when we moved to the house that needed nothing.

Water lands over all in a wash of sound. Overflowing
    swoosh rumbles
like freeway traffic yet no freeway resides. No travelers
    wander
deserted beachside drives. The full width and sweep of
    the horizon
fills with sound and you power-up planers, saws and
    sanders
to enhance the house that needed nothing.

Smacks of rain knuckle the roof, windows and doors. A
    cacophony
unlike songs of carillon bells, babies laughing, or the
    feeling
you have when you look at lemon Jell-O. The opposite of
    what you think
when you think of meditation, or fresh gardenias, or a
    blue pool
of calm when chocolate melts in your mouth, but new
    rooms'

elegant chests of drawers, dinning room chairs and table,
    and the faithful
balance of the tall case clock constructed in your shop
    gradually,
amplify our home that needed nothing more than us.

The Most Important Thing to Save When the House is Burning Down

Save George. Save the way he says *bow wow*
as he greets his crush of dogs.
Save how he rolls on the floor, three dogs
clambering over him licking his beard.
How he laughs and how all four of them
make those snuggling noises.
Save George when he is excited
and lifts his heels bobbing
off the floor, sometimes
drops of spittle sparkle in the corner
of his lips while he tells stories
and can't talk fast enough.
His cut hands are calloused,
raw from working wood.
Save the way he looks at them and shrugs.
Save George who never looks at dirt,
the worst person to clean house.
You can save him regardless—
as you follow him around to find
what messes he misses—
but watch, he can't pass
the coffee table without setting
each item in the spot
he insists it must be. Methodically
he moves the Deco birchwood box
an eighth of an inch, straightens
the album, exacting edge to edge.
Don't forget
to save the way he walks room
to room brushing his teeth.
Even if you find the toothbrush
abandoned on the kitchen counter or top

of the dresser, save it.
He is a hugger.
That is the most important thing to save
when the house is burning down.
Save his hugs and how, when he hugs,
he says—that's nice
I needed that.

A Long Marriage

A verbal solo
　　accompanies every
　　　　action: a *toot tooter,*
　　　　　　a *yu-hooer,* an *oh-my-oh my-er,*
　　sounds out *pooh!* with puckered lips

he's a noise maker.
　　Audible *sigher,*
　　　　tongue *clucker.*
　　　　　　Often *woo-woo-who* on an ascending scale
　　　　　　hitched
　　　　　　　　to words inaudible below
breath cussing discussing lamenting venting,
in sleep he sings, laughs, converses
in song lyrics from the jazz age and
she's an age

desperate
　　to be surrounded by
　　　　blue space of quiet
　　　　　　inside her head

　　craving
　　　　ambiance
　　　　　　silent as clouds
　　　　　　　　to navigate
　　　　　　　　　create,

the better to hear in serenity
　　herself
　　　　think as if wrapped in a warm
　　　　　　blanket.

Crossing path's paradox
    on their own orbits
they're married, of course
as every evening the sound
she adores
encircles her.
        Oh love you love you just love you!

Where We Are Now

Neither one of us remember anything this nice judge said
"take you"
"wife"/"husband"/
"this day"/
"better"/
"worse"/"rich"/
"poor"/"sick"/
"healthy"/
"to love"/
"cherish"

"until death"—did we repeat? And now on this exact spot
transmogrified by time
you who witnessed
thirty-seven years ago
and those of you
who did not, gather
with us here to foster
our future
promises/

from where, relative to then/ we are now

I promise/
to listen
before
I respond I promise/
to respect
your idiosyncrasies
whenever
I notice them I promise/
to continue

to relish little
and large
absurdities of life
with laughter.
If necessary I
promise/ to endeavor,
to find courage

to make hard decisions.
I promise/ to
love/ promise
to cherish/ you/
as I have done until
now, and until neither of us can remember anything

About the Author

Carol Levin's motto is "The more information you have the more choices you have."

Long ago, her information gathering began by studying, performing and teaching modern dance. She served as the artistic director of a small company. Later, completed the college curriculum for radio broadcasting, and was on-air as the morning drive-time DJ playing jazz, blues, and news reports.

Along the way, she's worked at a children's hospital as the "Employment Manager." She studied acting at Freehold Theatre Lab/Studio in Seattle and The American Contemporary Theater (ACT) in San Francisco, which led her to train and certify as an Alexander Technique International Certified Teacher.

She spent twenty years as a supernumerary (silent actor) in Seattle Opera productions. Then in the years she was a founding member and Literary Manager of the Art Theatre of Puget Sound, she translated, along with two Russians, Anton Chekhov's four major plays and a Dictionary of Stanislavski Terms for Theater artists.

Also, she has a lot of information about yoga and of course, writing poetry.

Levin has published two full volumes of poetry, *Confident Music Would Fly Us to Paradise* (MoonPath Press, 2014), and *Stunned By the Velocity* (Pecan Grove Press 2012). Also, two chapbooks, *Red Rooms and Others* (Pecan Grove Press, 2009), and *Sea Lions Sing Scat* (Finishing Line Press 2007).

Recent poems appear in *The Poeming Pigeon, A Literary Journal of Poetry, The Literary Nest,* and World Enough Writers' *Ice Cream Poems Anthology.* Her work's been widely published in journals and anthologies, print and online, in Russia, New Zealand, Germany, UK, and the US.

She is Editorial Assistant at the journal, *Crab Creek Review* in Seattle. She also teaches The Breathing Lab / Alexander Technique. www.the-breathing-lab.com

Carol has another motto too: "Surround yourself with excellence, it brings out the best in you."

CPSIA information can be obtained
at www.ICGtesting.com
Printed in the USA
LVHW03s0029060818
586084LV00002B/249/P

9 781936 657384